Truly a book for all seasons, *Unwrapping His Presence* is full of wonderful surprises. Suggestion: Plan to read it with pen and paper in reach. If you're like me, you'll find yourself pausing to jot down phrases, sentences, and ideas to remember, savor, and share with others. The author is a gifted writer who gently elicits every emotion—from smile to tear—from his readers.

—Holly Miller,
Contributing Editor of *The Saturday Evening Post* Author of more than a dozen books

Chris Maxwell's poetic gift of "reproducing a world in a word" has never been more obvious than in his latest book, *Unwrapping His Presence—What We Really Need for Christmas.* Chris eloquently relates Christmas in three basic truths: God came; God came in an unexpected way; God came in an unexpected moment. *Unwrapping His Presence* reminds us that as it was then, so it is now! In the diverse, often unhappy circumstances of a frenzied and frustrating Christmas, the glorious gift of God's Presence can be unwrapped in unexpected ways at unexpected moments. You can help a friend "Unwrap His Presence" if you will wrap this book up as a present this Christmas!

—Dr. Ronald W. Carpenter, Sr.,
Presiding Bishop, International Pentecostal Holiness Church

Unwrapping His Presence serves to do just that. The prose, the rhymes, the pain, the promise, the memories, the ecstasy, the profundity, the calamity, the simplicity, the complexity, the wonder, the disbelief, the exuberance, the disappointment, the promise, the Presence…it's all here. You can't read these lines without rehearsing your own stories and re-living your own life scenes. Each page beckons us to pause and ponder, wait and welcome, encounter and embrace—to receive again so we might give it away…again. As I read these pages I sensed both the Presence of my beloved Jesus and the presence of Chris, my dear friend. Both melted my heart, amazed my mind, and motivated my will to allow His Presence to course through me to those far from Him…Mary Christmas, indeed!

> —C. Tracy Reynolds,
> Dean, School of Christian Ministries, Emmanuel College
> Leadership & Assimilation Pastor
> Grace Fellowship

Chris Maxell is one part poet and two parts story-teller. So it's no surprise that his latest book, *Unwrapping His Presence—What We Really Need for Christmas* is a joy to read. Take a day off from the hustle and bustle, settle into an easy chair and read this book. I have no doubt you'll soon be enjoying the Holy presence of Jesus.

> —Gary W. Moon, Editor of the *Conversations Journal*
> Author, *Apprenticeship with Jesus*

My friend Chris Maxwell is a literary troubadour. He's part poet, part musician, and part theologian. Yet he crafts his words like a prophet—or maybe a surgeon—and penetrates hearts so he can change people inside. When writing about Christmas, he helps us see how we have trivialized the celebration, and he beckons us to embrace authenticity. He cuts away the superficial and takes us to the core of what Christ's birth is really all about.

> —J. Lee Grady
> Author, *The Holy Spirit Is Not for Sale*

Real beauty is complex and multifaceted. This is why beauty has inspired all aspects of art from songs to poetry to the canvas. Chris Maxwell offers to help us explore the deepest beauty of all…the incarnation which is the glory of God shown in the face of Christ. Chris guides us into the depths of the beauty of Christmas using the entire toolbox of art. It is an invitation you can't afford to pass up.

> —Joe Coffey
> Lead Pastor of Hudson Community Chapel
> Author, *Red Like Blood*

Unwrapping His Presence is a much-needed, thoughtful reflection on a holy season that in our culture offers little opportunity for contemplation. Chris Maxwell's elegant writing provides that opportunity, by allowing readers to take a deep breath, spend a few moments in quiet reflection, and let God's presence infuse and refresh their lives.

> —Marcia Ford, author of *Traditions of the Ancients: Vintage Faith Practices for the 21st Century*

In the past year, I was introduced to Chris Maxwell. What I appreciate about Chris I have also discovered between the pages of *Unwrapping His Presence*. This book, like its author, is warm, direct, and authentic. I encourage you to invest some time this Christmas season (and beyond) discovering these simple moments of reflection.

—Eddie Taylor
President, Family Discipleship Ministries
Husband, father of three sons, pastor, and speaker

Christmas is a time of wonder and celebration, but for many people, it is a time of sorrow and of grief. Chris Maxwell has captured both the celebration and the reflection that IS Christmas. This book is filled with inspirational stories that will encourage the heart, yet while reading the pages of *Unwrapping His Presence*, one will look inward for personal renewal. The central focus of the book is on the *gift* given at Christmas as well as the Giver.

—Dr. Michael S. Stewart
President, Emmanuel College
Franklin Springs, GA

Chris Maxwell has done it again! The sharp yet seasoned words penetrate our minds and hearts with emotionally packed insights of the Christmas Season. His inclusion of Mary DeMent's writings adds to the joy this book brings. Reading this book during the Advent Season is a great way to settle your heart and mind in the busyness of Christmas.

—Dr. A. D. Beacham, Jr
Executive Director, IPHC World Missions Ministries
Oklahoma City, OK

It's easy to miss the high drama of the Christmas story. We think we know it from our repeated hearing. And we may conclude that we have its larger message down pat, but Chris knows well that the Bible account of God made Human resounds with surprising turns and unexpected insights. He eloquently helps us see what was there all along but maybe we missed. He helps us experience the Gift anew, and may just help this year's holiday to be a more truly holy day.

> —Timothy Jones, Episcopal minister and author of *The Art of Prayer: A Simple Guide to Conversation with God*

Ironically, the Christmas season can be a period of pain and mental anguish for many. Heartrending memories often resurface making it a challenge just to cope. Chris Maxwell in his newest book, *Unwrapping His Presence*, offers solace and solution to all who are grief laden and troubled. With his unique storytelling gift, Chris challenges the reader to seek God's unfailing presence and tackle problems with grace and resolve. I heartily recommend it as a must read, especially for those entering the Advent season with pain and disillusionment. You won't be disappointed!

> —Dr. John Chasteen
> Executive Director, Southwestern Christian University's LifeCoaching Institute

Chris Maxwell's words sing on every page as he reminds us not just of the "reason for the season" but the reason why God still matters in a sin-darkened world—every day of the year.

> —A.J. Kiesling, author of *Jaded: Hope for Believers Who Have Given Up on Church but Not on God* (Revell)

Poetic reflections of hope that communicate the thoughts and feelings of the heart we all might experience during the holidays. The stories and words translate into insightful truths that will add threads to the fabric of your faith.

—Tim Kuck
COO & Executive VP, Regal Boats
President, Nathaniel's Hope

If you are tired of the same old routine for Christmas, this is the book you have been waiting for. *Unwrapping His Presence* opens the door to set you free from the stress, guilt, and boredom of Christmas. It is one of the most authentic, powerful, insightful books on embracing pain and grief during the Christmas season. Maxwell has a knack for helping you see things in a totally different perspective you would not have otherwise thought of. *Unwrapping His Presence* will help you understand sickness and the purpose of grief. This is the Christmas gift idea of the year. It will inspire and empower you to a deeper appreciation for living life to its fullest. This book is a must read.

—Kore Liow, MD, FACP, FAAN
Neurologist and Epileptologist, Director, Hawaii Pacific Neuroscience
Clinical Professor of Neurology, University of Hawaii John Burns School of Medicine

Unwrapping His Presence is a beautiful blend of prose and poetry! Let Chris Maxwell's insight refresh and strengthen you. Let his heart deeply motivate you to love God and others during this season of Grace. Let his words calm and inspire you as he unwraps the profound meaning of the Christ Child.

> —Dr. Trevor Francis
> University of Arkansas
> Author of *Try Higher: The Call to Every College Student*

What a reflective, poetic, and intimate insight into the miracle of Christmas. Chris Maxwell, along with contributions from Mary DeMent, has done a masterful job of assisting us with embracing the wonder of this Holy time and bringing His Presence into our every day challenges. I will never approach Christmas the same after reading this gift of words.

> —Dennis Wells
> Counselor & Author

Unwrapping His Presence opened my eyes to another facet of the holiday season and of faith in Christ. It's easy to get lost in the busyness of Christmas. With the heart of a pastor, Chris Maxwell gently challenged me to look beyond the hustle and bustle of the season, to experience the very essence of Christ's presence, and through the eyes of a Savior see past the exterior of mankind and into its soul. This new book is one you'll want to share with friends and family. You'll stop and reflect many times at the deep wisdom presented so simply and beautifully by this compassionate and genuine lover of God and people.

> —Hope Hammond
> Woman, wife, mother, minister, recording artist
> Founder, Emerge with Hope, Blogger, *Journey of Hope*

Chris Maxwell gives a "Changing My Mind" to Christmas! His book allows his readers to connect to hurts and losses in their lives, while giving hope and practical advice to foster healing! The advice he and Mrs. DeMent give is sound and true for those who are looking for hope during the Christmas season! Chris allows Jesus to be at the heart of why He came to earth, to heal those who are hurting. Chris not only identifies with those who are broken, but he beckons them to embark on the journey to wholeness through Christ! This isn't just a book, but it is a bringer of peace, hope, and joy!

—Blake Rackley, Psy.D.
Assistant Professor of Psychology, Emmanuel College
Clinical Psychology Resident

Any time I read what Chris shares, I always feel encouraged to know that another pilgrim on our life's journey has been where I've been or has been where I'm going. I can always relate and learn. I appreciate what Chris shares and his honesty in describing how it felt, what it looked like, or what he learned. Chris Maxwell is real. Especially during the Christmas season, that is a refreshing comfort and an inspiring reminder of how we can travel through life together as Jesus travels with us.

—Paula K. Dixon
Believer, wife, mom, friend
Emmanuel College Faculty
Franklin Springs, Georgia

Christmas can mean different things to many people. Created by God for the purposes of worship and fellowship, the reader is transported back in time. Chris Maxwell takes us on a journey as only he can by reliving Jesus' story in light of the true meaning of Christmas. Chris combines poetry with extraordinary story telling. Through these pages, I could smell the food, see the lights, and hear the chorals from days gone by at Christmas. I was prodded to reach back and discover for myself once again what Christmas is all about. Christmas is about reflection and the birth of Christ. Chris makes sure we never forget what Christmas means- that being Christ at the center of every present and presence.

> —Chip B. Furr, husband, father, dreamer, visionary, and author of *Thin Places—Surprising Collisions Between the Human Spirit and the Presence of God*; CLIMB, Founder and President

Unwrapping HIS Presence

Unwrapping HIS Presence

Chris Maxwell
with stories by **Mary DeMent**

artwork by BRENT CHITWOOD

HIGHERLIFE
DEVELOPMENT SERVICES, INC

Oviedo, Florida

Unwrapping His Presence—What We Really Need for Christmas
by Chris Maxwell with stories by Mary DeMent
Artwork by Brent Chitwood

Published by HigherLife Development Services, Inc.
400 Fontana Circle
Building 1 – Suite 105
Oviedo, Florida 32765
(407) 563-4806
www.ahigherlife.com

ISBN 13: 978-1-935245-39-1
ISBN 10: 1-935245-39-2

Cover Design: r2c Design—Rachel Lopez

First Edition

10 11 12 13 — 9 8 7 6 5 4 3 2 1

Printed in the United States of America

Table of Contents

Acknowledgments

My Creator for His ideas, His love, His acceptance, and His forgiveness.

My Family: Debbie, Taylor, Brittany, Anthem, Aaron, and Graham. Thanks for joining me in the experience of learning this thing called life. Thanks for the gifts of being yourselves.

To my father and my sisters, and everyone in our family. Mama would be singing to us all right now.

Mary, for your willingness to include your stories. Your writing is like an artist displaying scenes through words.

Brent, for your willingness to include your artwork. Your creativity reveals in image what our words hope to draw.

Paul, for your editing. You understand poetry, prose, and poetic prose. You keep rhythm and flow while making the writer look better. You know when to provide surgery and when a little makeup is enough.

Dave, for allowing me to write and edit for you. And for letting these stories be unwrapped for Christmas.

To the faculty, staff, students, and alumni of Emmanuel College: I am honored to talk about Emmanuel the school, and Emmanuel the God who refuses to leave us alone.

To my accountability partners, editors, writers, authors, musicians, artists, friends, and those who have allowed me the honor of serving as their pastor. Thanks for singing life to me in a variety of ways over so many years.

To all of my friends with epilepsy, this book is especially for you. Let us all receive the Gift, as we grasp every moment this Christmas season.

Foreword

Standing and Waiting

One night, after ball games and the Children's Christmas Musical rehearsal, we bought a tree. A green tree that stood waiting. We purchased, cut, placed, and watered. We began clothing and coloring, while keeping the water stand full.

Many nights, after days of giving and receiving, I feel like a tree. Standing. Waiting. I relax, though, remembering I've been purchased, cut, placed, and watered. My Joyful Owner clothes and colors me, while keeping the water stand full.

Many people feel like trees waiting to be wanted. During this December, I pray they recall a real meaning behind the meals and melodies. I pray they find clothes and colors for their inner selves gladly given by their True Owner. If so, they shall never run dry.

The Tree Maker stands waiting.

These pages will help us notice.

Introduction

Taken

Christmas. Many of us share common thoughts about this time of year. Each of us also has a few memories that belong only to us.

As Christians, we talk about remembering the true meaning of this season. We fuss about Jesus being left out. We then find ourselves trapped in the rush of our own holiday hurry. We notice very little difference between ourselves and those whose beliefs we debate.

God, though, has a suggestion. He wants us to take time to take His Holy Presence, wrapped below our hurried flow of chores and choirs and dinners, and unwrap it. As we find Him, we find Him to be just what we need.

The following stories will help us do that. These words and pages will challenge our choices. They will remind us of Christian beliefs about Christ's birth, merging that event into the middle of our rapid sprint through the season.

Poetic stories will help us pause, glance, and receive the best gift available.

Though the season is packed, we can make room in our inns to find Him. On these pages, He is revealed and unwrapped. God is ours for the taking. We are then His for the remaking.

> That is truly the greatest gift of all.
> Let us take Him. Let us be taken by Him.

—Chris Maxwell

Chapter

1

Listen: A Word to the World

"But you, Bethlehem Ephrathah,
though you are small among the clans of Judah,
out of you will come for me
one who will be ruler over Israel,
whose origins are from of old,
from ancient times."

—Micah 5:2

The tilted planet spins by habit in sad silence. Heaven is quiet. No words have fallen from above for four still centuries.

Will earth end this way? Will she slow, sleep, die while her Maker appears absent?

Creator spoke in days past. His voice through creation, His voice through creatures, came clearly. Words thundered, whispered, burned into the conscience of this populated satellite.

The words stopped. People noise continued: words scattered, words sent, words screamed around the earth and up from earth toward the squelched sky. But from above, nothing.

She flies through skies on course: a planet in place on a pause of maintenance. Can she keep going while weighted with the heavy silence? Will her malaise catch and moor her?

This cannot be all. Creator promised to say more. The Father of worlds vowed to voice His word again.

Tonight, some say, the silence has ceased.

Tonight, some say, the Word has come.

Wrapped in swaddling clothes, lying in a manger, some say, the Word has come.

Sound waves of infant cries: Could it be the voice of God? Shepherds and sheep, mom and dad and angels gather around the center of attention. A Baby born in a world hoping to hear from heaven: Is such a small event worth so much attraction?

God would speak from a mountain or a temple or a television studio. God would speak as a religious leader or a king or a political activist. Not from a barn as a Baby.

The signs shout and dare a world to believe.

Dark doubt has lost a little of its grip on earth tonight, for some reason. The planet of frowns has found a few smiles of wonder tonight, for some reason.

Will a world hear a Word and be healed? Hear a word from an Infant and find faith? Will she?

Time will tell. But tonight the sky is scattered with sound. The music of angels, of stars, of promises fulfilled.

It does appear odd that God would talk this way. And after so long. Yet, if this is God, pray the planet shall listen.

Shall listen, as she spins and flies through noisy skies, shall listen. Pray she shall hear that a long-awaited Word is here.

Christmas is all about wonder, a time when men and angels marvel at the goodness of a God who would leave heaven to rescue us.

—J. Lee Grady

Chapter 2

Baby: A Christmas Cry

But when the time arrived that was set by God the Father, God sent his Son, born among us of a woman, born under the conditions of the law so that he might redeem those of us who have been kidnapped by the law. Thus we have been set free to experience our rightful heritage. You can tell for sure that you are now fully adopted as his own children because God sent the Spirit of his Son into our lives crying out, "Papa! Father!" Doesn't that privilege of intimate conversation with God make it plain that you are not a slave, but a child? And if you are a child, you're also an heir, with complete access to the inheritance.

— Galatians 4:4–7 (THE MESSAGE)

i am an infant,
crawling around on the floor.
staring up

at the stairway,
i long to rise;
stand, walk, run, climb,
ascend to the top
and meet God.
but i am a baby,
incapable of such a feat.

God is there.
i am here.

the ten steps,[*]
stone stairs that offer access to God
are too formidable;
i am too weak, too immature.
God speaks from the majestic height:
He has heard my cries.
He sends a Rescuer
who descends the stairs,
a Giant shrinking in size
as He nears the bottom.
i am shocked, stunned.
when He arrives at the floor
He is an infant
crawling with me.

He has become like me.
but how will we climb the steps
and arrive at the place of our longing?

---

[*] The Ten Commandments

somehow this Babe lifts me up.
one step. then two. then another.
pushing and straining;
i see what is happening:
He is slowly dying,
exhausting His energy
by powering me to the top.

i arrive at God's presence
full of sadness and joy;
i sing for me and hurt for the Rescuer.

i see God.
i see God.

i think i know Him.
i think He knows me.

He smiles.
i cry.
His smile looks similar to a Baby's.
my cry is now the cry of a man.

> *At Christmas, God decided to become more than a
> scratch and sniff book; He bursts into the world of
> my five senses.*

—Joe Coffey

Grief: Journey Through

He shall feed his flock like a shepherd: he shall gather the lambs with his arm, and carry them in his bosom, and shall gently lead those that are with young.

—Isaiah 40:11 (KJV)

The family never spent Christmas that way before. They would never spend it that way again. Opening presents and eating meals couldn't turn their minds toward holiday gusto. Not that year. Tears replaced laughter. Fears flavored moods.

Carolyn, whose humor normally decorated seasonal scenes, stayed in bed. Silent. Doctors and nurses had lost hope, releasing her into the care of family. Her husband,

Bill, took her to their daughter's apartment. As Christmas came, Carolyn's consciousness left.

How could a family face that crisis? They did what she would have wanted. They played songs of the season. Displayed red and green colors? Ate sweet food? Yes, as they sang and prayed near a silent mother snuggled in her bed. Still. No normal giggles and jokes came from her mouth. Just breaths. And those were slowly fading.

Two days after Christmas, Bill's tearful words gave the news: "Come see your mother again. She has left us. But, she feels better now."

Her life would never leave their minds. They had prayed, believing for healing. Their knowledge of God reminded them that heaven brought healing, that no more chemotherapy would be needed, that no more hair would be lost, that no longer would her voice be silent.

But, that biblical therapy did not remove their grief. Shifting gears from numbness, to sadness, to anger, to denial, to questions, their journey was not pleasant. Carolyn's baby-of-the-family felt tiny as he, a nineteen-year-old Bible college student, drove two hours back home. Alone. No music. No words. No Mama. Only 120 silent minutes that seemed to shout more loudly than any carolers. His life would never be the same.

Like that family, many people gather together during December facing pain. Death counts, test results, and obituary columns almost shout. Cancer, HIV, terrorist attacks, heart attacks, anthrax, car crashes, suicide, rage, age. Causes vary, while lives on earth conclude. Sadness settles nearby for friends. People ask, "Why?"

On holiday journeys through change, are we really alone? How can we find help for grief and loneliness? Our beliefs announce that God listens to those who cry.

Karen, a nurse who cares for the sick, trusts God's care. Decembers remind Karen of when her husband died beside her.

Karen handles the holidays by praying with honesty, remembering God isn't offended by questions. She stays busy quilting and cross-stitching. She reads the Bible, although she remembers, "It seemed strange to read alone." Conversations with nurses from work, friends from church, and family members help. Karen says, "Talking about my husband and how he died let me deal with my grief."

Karen also found ways to encourage others instead of waiting for all hurt to depart. She says, "I bought toys for a ministry that helps grieving children. My husband loved children and always gave. The director's husband had died several years ago. She welcomed my words of pain. I also offered a listening ear as a nurse. Just my care helped families of our patients who died."

Helping them helped Karen. Reaching out, releasing feelings, and receiving spiritual therapy reminded Karen she wasn't alone at all. Her Father would never leave or forsake her.

Dr. Richard Dobbins has learned God can help in our seasons of sadness. He says,

> In this life, there are some things we will never understand. The enemy can use those questions to make you bitter and to turn you away from God if you let him. But know that God is the one who can truly comfort you and give you the peace and grace to survive your tragedy.*

While not understanding causes, people who miss others during this time can stand under the greatest source of help available. Busy sidewalks and silent nights bring pain. As we cry, we can pursue peace from God.

---

* (Copyright © 2001 Dr. Richard D. Dobbins, Founder and President of EMERGE Ministries, Inc. Akron, Ohio, in partnership with Media Ministries of the Assemblies of God. Reprinted with permission. "DayForward Online with Dr. Richard D. Dobbins" is a radio ministry of Media Ministries of the Assemblies of God, Springfield, Missouri.)

Joe ministers as a pastor, hoping to touch businessmen, seekers, and traditional believers. He also remembers his younger brother dying on a motorcycle.

Teresa tried desperately to heal her husband of cancer. Trips to other countries. Prayers. Praise songs. Natural medicine and proper diets. Still, her house is empty now. This December she still misses Guy.

Eve stopped a wedding rehearsal and postponed her wedding. The reason? Her brother died in December of 1955. Holiday moments and anniversary discussions make that date still feel recent.

Stan remembers his father's funeral in a church auditorium decorated with Christmas scenery. As his eyes observed the seasonal colors, his ears heard "Joy to the World" and "Oh, Come All Ye Faithful," and a sermon about a dad really being "Home for the Holidays."

Doug preaches globally. Each Christmas he writes a new story, reminding readers and hearers of a Miracle that came here. In December, he wishes his parents could join him near a decorated tree.

This Christmas, a couple will again think of twins that never lived to see wrapped gifts. This Christmas, many people will think of family members and friends who didn't know in advance that a September in America would change them and the world forever. This Christmas, though, the Birthday Boy now serves as King, promising to bring the greatest gift of all to those who ask: His Presence.

He gladly eats with, sings with, and cries with those in need of a friend.

Bill still thinks of Carolyn. Janet and Laura never stop missing their mother. And their brother, Chris, writes stories like this while still wishing his mother could sing Christmas songs to his three sons and his grandson. But he knows the Doctor who brings peace—not always instead of pain, often amid pain. Dose by dose, through the medicine of songs sung and journals kept and words prayed, help and healing come. Often with tears. Frequently with fullness of joy.

I know it to be true. I am that Chris. My eyes watched my mom Carolyn—the comedian, the cook, the example of life—slowly sink from cancer. Now, though I have lived longer with her gone than with her near, I still miss her. My choice? To rejoice though weeping, to release while sad, to receive by giving. That is how she would have liked it.

Isn't that what a manger and a star and a journey of kings remind us of anyway?

Faith and hope can flavor this year's moods. Colors and foods have deeper meanings if we eat and look while tasting and seeing the Lord's goodness—that greatest Gift of all. Unwrapping that Presence, decorating symbolism with reality, doing unto others who need us this December— healing will come to those who share hurt and hope for Christmas.

That is what Carolyn, my mother, would have me do.

That is what Christ, my Savior, can do for us and through us.

So, come. Let us adore Him, knowing, on this journey, we are not alone after all.

Great little One! whose all-embracing birth
Lifts Earth to Heaven, stoops Heaven to Earth.

—Richard Crashaw[1]

Counselor and writer Mary DeMent understands seasonal reminders of loss. On the seventeenth anniversary of her father's death, she offers these suggestions:

- Write about a favorite holiday memory you and your loved one shared.
- Donate flowers "in memory of" to your local church.
- Visit their gravesite. Decorate it with flowers. Pray for yourself and other relatives or friends.
- Invite the family to share a memory they have of the deceased. (You might actually learn something you never knew.)

- Look through old photos/albums/videos, remembering times together.
- Review old journal entries you wrote during the beginning stages of your grief.
- Revisit a place you went with the deceased. Remember a special time. Share your memory with someone else.
- Write about how you're feeling right now:

  - What do you wish you could change?
  - What do you wish you could have said or done?
  - How have you changed since the loss?
  - What are your fears? hopes? dreams?
  - Have realistic expectations for yourself.

Chapter
4

Remember: A Way Toward the Manger

This is how the birth of Jesus Christ came about: His mother Mary was pledged to be married to Joseph, but before they came together, she was found to be with child through the Holy Spirit. Because Joseph her husband was a righteous man and did not want to expose her to public disgrace, he had in mind to divorce her quietly.

But after he had considered this, an angel of the Lord appeared to him in a dream and said, "Joseph son of David, do not be afraid to take Mary home as your wife, because what is conceived in her is from the Holy Spirit. She will give birth to a son, and you are to give him the name Jesus, because he will save his people from their sins."

All this took place to fulfill what the Lord had said through the prophet: "The virgin will be with child and will give birth to a son, and they will call him Immanuel"—which means, "God with us."

— Matthew 1:18–23

Then.

Away in a manger. That's where they were.

A young Mary. An unsure Joseph. A baby Jesus within, soon to be born.

The outcome? We sing it this season. We declare it with reason.

Now.

Away are the strangers. That's where they are.

A sick mother. A crippled father. A baby breathing his last, soon to depart.

The outcome? They hurt this season. They despise it for a reason.

What should we do? How can the ones with homes give gifts and time and love to the homeless? How can the well send healthy smiles and listening ears to the sick?

So many Marys and Josephs and soon-to-be-born babies need homes. So many walkers and talkers need hope.

So many religious experts need truth. So many crying humans need tender loving care.

Start it at home, sending gifts of kindness to those so close? Steer it toward unlikely places, offering presents of true Christian joy to those bathed in hurt? Encourage the down? Feed the hungry?

Many rooms and roads help the lonely hide. May I— may we—run toward them this season. Let's visit a prison. Let's take time to give a smile to a rushing shopper. Let's surprise a missionary with money. Let's offer an hour of listening to an elderly talker. Let's drive the wheelchair of a friend who remembers her days as a walker.

Can we give gifts to a prisoner's child through Angel Tree?* Can we sing songs at hospitals with a ministry like Nathaniel's Hope**?

A smile. A prayer. A song. A gift. Yes, there are ways. Many ways.

---

* Angel Tree is a ministry that reaches out to the children of inmates and their families with the love of Christ. This unique program gives your church an opportunity to share Christ's love by helping to meet the physical, emotional, and spiritual needs of the families of prisoners. www.angeltree.org.

** Nathaniel's Hope is an outreach of Teams Commissioned for Christ Int'l (TCCI), a non-profit, 501 (c) (3) Christian missions organization dedicated to sharing hope with kids with special needs (VIP kids) and their families. wwwnathanielshope.org.

On these days, remember the manger. And don't let a stranger get away.

Are you willing to forget what you have done for other people, and to remember what other people have done for you...to remember the weakness and loneliness of people who are growing old...Are you willing to believe that love is the strongest thing in the world—stronger than hate, stronger than evil, stronger than death...Then you can keep Christmas... But you can never keep it alone.

—Henry Van Dyke[2]

Chapter

5

Wanted: The Best Part of Christmas

By Mary DeMent

Jesus replied: "Love the Lord your God with all your heart and with all your soul and with all your mind." This is the first and greatest commandment.

— Matthew 22:37, 38

The time away with my husband was nice. We enjoyed uninterrupted meals and conversation. Sanity returned. But I was anxious to reunite with my children. I loved seeing their faces as we walked in the door. The feeling appeared mutual.

After the babysitter left and the initial hug, kiss and tickle fest was over, I sat down on the couch with my oldest, who was three at the time. This stay-at-home Mom had been away from her "job" for over twenty-four hours. Input was crucial. What did they do all of that time? Did they have fun? I needed a debriefing.

The sitter had previously informed me of their activities. I knew their needs were met and that they enjoyed their day. They played inside and out, ate well, napped well, and even went for a wagon ride. But the Mom in me needed to know more.

So, I sat down with my son, the informer, and asked him, "What was the best part of your day?" He thought for a moment, gave me that grin of his and said, "You!" I don't have to tell you how that made me feel. But I will. I was overjoyed. I thought, "I must be the happiest Mom in the world!" To think that those brief moments spent tickling, hugging, and kissing meant more to him than any other moment of his fun-filled day was overwhelming to me.

Then I considered God. He desires to know about our day, our likes, our dislikes, our joys, and our disappointments. He wants a debriefing on our lives, emotions, thoughts, and activities. He longs to spend "couch time" with His children. Daily. In the morning, in the evening, and in between. Time of day is really irrelevant.

My thoughts shifted to Christmastime. 'Tis the season to be busy. Busy with parties and planning. Busy with family and friends. Or maybe we're busy unwrapping all the unwanted emotions the holidays sometimes impart to us.

Whatever the case, allow me to add one more event to your packed calendar. Make time to sit down on the couch with your Father. It may be after the last guest leaves, after the last present is opened, or after the last tear is shed. But please sit with Him. Reflect on the events of the day, the month. And when He asks, "What was the best part of your Christmas?" why not make Him the happiest Dad in the world?

> *Christmas is not as much about opening our presents as opening our hearts.*
>
> —Janice Maeditere[3]

Pausing: Comfort and Joy

Why are you downcast, O my soul? Why so disturbed within me? Put your hope in God, for I will yet praise him, my Savior and my God.

— Psalm 42:11

early in December my wife celebrates her birthday. In the month's middle, my middle son enjoys his.

Christmas comes and goes. A new year arrives and picks up speed.

During the final month, weeks, days of this year, what are our plans? Will we purchase and pack, give and receive, eat and enjoy? Will we laugh or cry? Will we drive or fly? Can we afford what we hope to buy?

Often, while rushing to get ahead, we get behind. The wrapping and the eating and the singing and the meeting pack calendars, leaving no room in our inns. We hide hurt; we deny truth; we lose that loving feeling.

Events of temporary worth rob time to invest in permanent value.

But we can change that. In the lovely weather and on the sleigh rides together, on a white Christmas, during our moments of stepping into Christmas, whether it is holly-jolly or merry, let us pause to notice the tidings of comfort and joy.

Comfort and joy. Even in a culture containing more jingle bell rocks than holy nights, even on calendars pasting more demands than we should pursue on the twelve days of Christmas, let us pause. Let us notice. Comfort. Joy. They are available, like stars of wonder, stars of light. Those choosing to pause and notice can then see what is waiting to be observed.

Comfort and joy. Don't you need those two gifts this year? Can't they calm you and thrill you? Even during noisy nights and seasons with war on earth, can't we receive the gifts of comfort and joy?

Stop rocking around the Christmas tree long enough to hear a voice asking this question: Do you hear what I hear?

Think about the question. Answer it. Then hear what is so near. Let us not ignore Him.

> *This is Christmas: not the tinsel, not the giving and receiving, not even the carols, but the humble heart that receives anew the wondrous gift, the Christ.*
>
> —Frank McKibben[4]

Transformation: Communicating the Word in a Changing Society— That Glorious Song of Old

May the God of peace, who through the blood of the eternal covenant brought back from the dead our Lord Jesus, that great Shepherd of the sheep, equip you with everything good for doing his will, and may he work in us what is pleasing to him, through Jesus Christ, to whom be glory for ever and ever. Amen.

— Hebrews 13:20-21

G o back in time. Travel to Azusa Street in last century's inaugural decade. A breeze blew. God communicated. An audience listened. Societies changed. An outpouring welcomed the world into a new spiritual environment.

Surely the leaders had a major plan. Their scheme? Lapel mics, rehearsed drama, and the most fashionable clothes in town. Palm Pilot and Power Point? Televangelism and talented musicians?

Those weren't the ingredients of that feast. Like at Pentecost, people waited. God came. God blew. History shifted eternally.

But what about us? How, in the now, can we receive Christ's love and send it on a trip down today's streets? How can the same breeze blow so that a MP3-style listening audience hears? A lesson from this month's music can guide us.

There's a Song in the Air

Common themes of the Christmas season saturate the songs we hear. Our ears listen to tunes telling us of snow or shepherds or Santa. An analysis of how songwriters design lyrics illustrates our task.

Songs relate their main story in verses. Then, they highlight the meaning with the well-known portion, the chorus. Many tunes also include a third component, the bridge, described by author-singer John Fischer as "a breather so the chorus sounds fresh again, like something to clean the musical palette between courses."[5]

Musician Charlie Peacock offers his insight: "The verse is usually written as a message/story which supports and leads up to the chorus lyric. The chorus usually contains the central idea around which the whole song is based. The bridge is most often used to elaborate on the theme or to fill in some component of the message/story that had previously been missing." [6]

When it's Christmas time in the city, the ring-a-lings around us expose common ground. Meals, presents, and colors hit the headlines, moving the main theme to the back page. But we still share so much with those who do not know the One whose birthday we celebrate. That is the chorus, like the portion of a song few can forget. Christians know it. Doubters and seekers and wonderers know it.

Why not follow Christ's example and sing the chorus with our world in the middle of this culture as society rapidly swings its moods? By feeding hungry people, by E-mailing hurried readers, by finding a key story that fits the scene of the year, we can connect. We can sing a chorus. They will welcome and join in. A sensible illustration from life, a person's brief testimony in the middle of a sermon, special music, or skits linked to a shared theme of a message they can find common ground. A storyteller mentioning light and salt didn't surprise Jesus' audience. His people could relate.

It's not enough to find common ground, though. Songs contain more than a chorus. Deep meanings—found in verses that lyrically bring life to the tune—tell the whole story.

Likewise, as we seek to reach today's people, we must never alter the truth. Apologetics must find a home in daily living. Theology must reflect more than denominational uniqueness. It must cling to crucial elements of faith.

We claim to know a Doctor who can heal, a Mechanic who can fix, a Rescuer who can find, a Singer who can sing. His song is, we contend, a song of healing, tune-up, and eternal rescue. It occurs, we argue, when mistake-makers become singers of a song that never changes its theme.

Hateful attacks toward those who delete the phrase, "Christmas season," won't convince or convert. The poor and the rich, the healthy and the sick all need a present we have. Getting attention and sending gifts of love are important. But if we ask them, "Do you see what I see?" they would have to say, "No." We must present to them what we truly see.

Field and Fountain, Moor and Mountain

The last part of song lyrics—the bridge—will do that. Play with that word: bridge. View a change in scenery. A bridge is commonly viewed as that which connects one piece of land with another. This year, let us build one, welcoming the well-known chorus with the verses of good news gospel. With a bridge, a go-between, an awakening and alerting to the true theme, we can offer directions toward the birthday party.

Hal Donaldson seeks ways to do that. I recall a Christmas season when Hal's Convoy of Hope accomplished it in Orlando. Food, medical care, fun, and gospel presentations hit the city on a December Saturday. Stomachs were fed. Souls were saved. A bridge was built.

Hal remembers: "Whenever I see the wave of response to the altar—like the one in Orlando—I'm reminded how desperate people are. They want someone to love them, a reason to live. Orlando's churches demonstrated Christ's love that day. People wept with repentance and joy."

Like Convoy leaders and common volunteers, we all can build bridges. How? By choice. By taking chances. By seeing needs and taking action.

Dr. A.D. Beacham, Jr., author and executive director of the IPHC World Missions, remembers his father's approach: "My most memorable aspect of this happened when I was a boy wanting a bike for Christmas. I woke up Christmas morning to find a note from my parents instead of a bike. The note read, 'Dear Son, This year we decided to help provide Christmas for missionaries rather than for ourselves. We know you wanted a bike. But we hope you understand. We did this in obedience to Christ.' I was disappointed, but knew it was the right thing to do. I have never forgotten. Each year it reminds me of what the GIFT is really about."

Oh Come, All Ye Faithful

Let us do that all year long. Like holiday songs connect the common with the miraculous, God calls us to sing His facts right in the face of regularity. In good moments. In difficult times. Singing with our lives, our love, our care, our courage.

Tim and Marie Kuck, of Nathaniel's Hope, spent their son's first Christmas in the hospital, praying for him, watching each breath. God let Nathaniel live much longer than many expected. But not as long as so many hoped.

During his few years on earth, and now each Christmas since Nathaniel's departure to heaven, Tim and Marie return to hospitals to help those feeling alone during the holidays. Cookies, carols, and prayers bring new, true hope to parents and workers. Past and ongoing struggles motivate the Kucks to share their care.

Let us use all possible methods to tell that old, old story in new, fresh ways. In understandable language, a listening audience will see what we see. The speedy pace of cyberspace can bless, not stress. It can allow new methods of mingling, mentoring and merging. We can sing through our actions of love, singing loudly enough to be heard around the world and downtown city streets, whispering softly enough to be listened to in forgotten neighborhoods and lonely villages. Singing seasonal verses by *living them* helps us find a common chorus to ultimately build that bridge of grace.

Each of us—whatever our history—can maintain a central truth, offer a message story, and then sing a bridge. With small group accountability and festivals of prayer, we travel the proper direction. With laptops nearby, phones in our pockets, and lyrics on a techno-dynamic screen, we might get attention. We might make contact. But, whatever we have, we must pray for a breeze to blow, for God to sing, for audiences to listen and join in, for selfish societies to change.

Let us build such a bridge. God will love the song.

> *The best one sentence reaction I have is to put Paul's statement in 2 Corinthians 8:9 into the form of a question: "Do I (or you) really KNOW the grace of our Lord Jesus Christ, that though he was rich, yet he became poor that we through his poverty might become rich?"*
>
> —Dr. George O. Wood

Chapter 8

Pain: Nathaniel's Story

In the beginning was the Word, and the Word was with God, and the Word was God. He was with God in the beginning. Through him all things were made; without him nothing was made that has been made.

— John 1:1–3

Nathaniel spent his first Christmas in a hospital. He received his holiday meal from a feeding tube. His parents, Tim and Marie Kuck, counted Christ's birthday as day 116 in this home away from home. Nathaniel's two sisters wished for a normal Christmas.

Marie tells the story: "Nathaniel battled the flu Christmas Eve, his health rapidly deteriorating. I held his sick body in the early hours of Christmas morning, asking God to keep him out of the hospital until we could have a brief Christmas with our two girls. They had sacrificed so much for their brother the past few months. But we had to bring Nathaniel to Urgent Care at Arnold Palmer Children's Hospital. He was admitted on Christmas morning."

They struggled not to throw a pity party. It wasn't easy. After all they had faced, the Kucks felt cheated. Sitting alone with Nathaniel on Christmas day, watching him struggle for life, Marie remembered, "Others enjoyed the holiday. Not us. We were trapped. I wanted to be the one to offer hope and encouragement at Christmas, but the tables were turned."

Doctors and nurses knew Nathaniel well. His problems covered a wide range of difficulties. He was put on a respirator for survival. He spent his first three months in the Neonatal Intensive Care Unit undergoing six procedures that kept him alive. Then they did major surgery on Nathaniel's skull to allow room for his brain to grow.

A year passed slowly. Hoping and praying Nathaniel would miraculously improve, the Kucks longed to spend the next holidays far from that hospital's Special Care Unit. Good news came to the Kucks when they knew he would not have to stay for his second Christmas. Still, Tim and Marie were lured back to provide ministry to those facing what the Kucks knew so well. This time they returned by choice. This time they hoped to sing reminders of Christmas' true meaning with gifts and gadgets of red and green.

They gathered together with friends and tiny Nathaniel to offer songs of encouragement and sweet food. They held hands. They prayed prayers. They celebrated a season with those feeling isolated, sad, and worried. Tim said, "We felt like we could identify with those in the hospital. We wanted to make a difference with the love of Christ. Even if only in a small but tangible way: a smile, a song, a prayer." If Nathaniel's visit with a nurse can sing more than a song, if Tim and Marie's willingness to hug a doctor who wonders what went wrong can open an aching spiritual heart, each of us can sing along.

Marie remembered, "It was moving to see how people were so touched. We brought encouragement and hope by doing so little. Through their tearstained eyes, I could see they appreciated not being alone. Also, I think the nurses were touched to see us return, knowing how difficult our journey had been. They wondered why we would ever come back.

A nurse of fifteen years explained, "No one had ever done anything like that on Christmas Day.

Linda, a respiratory therapist, said, "Some of the staff still talk about it. One nurse says she'll never forget it. It's the most wonderful thing someone could have ever done on Christmas."

Nurses, doctors, patients, and relatives who saw Nathaniel the Christmas before heard much more than his family and friends singing seasonal songs. Such acts of love connected them with the true purpose of that holy day.

The Kucks continue letting their situation open more doors for them to help others. Even with Nathaniel now singing in heaven, Tim and Marie's ministry, Nathaniel's Hope, continues the tradition.

Can't we all join the Kucks? Even during holidays of need, isn't it healthy to notice the needs of others?

Let's give it a try. Praying and singing, even through pain gives a Great Gift to people wishing for a normal Christmas. It just might help them receive what they need the most.

> *Nearly every moment of every day we have the opportunity to give something to someone else— our time, our love, our resources. I have always found more joy in giving when I did not expect anything in return.*
>
> —S. Truett Cathy

Chapter

9

Love: A Christmas
I Remember

*You are the salt of the earth. But if the salt loses its
saltiness, how can it be made salty again? It is no
longer good for anything, except to be thrown out
and trampled by men.*

— Matthew 5:13

Dear Mama,

I miss you. How many years now? I have trouble remembering.
I have no trouble remembering you, though. Forever.

That cancer came and left and came again. You cared and
lived and then, after an energetic testimony of facing pain as a
true Christian, you left us for a better home.

Laughter. That was you. You did not depend on the assistance
of humorous stories and silly jokes. Your giggles came as a gift.
Your smile, your eyes, your joy. You knew how to laugh.

Love. That was you. You did not require the perfection of those around you. Your charity overcame so much pain. Your selfless-ness, your words, your listening ears. You knew how to love.

Life. That was you. You did not search for frail attempts at achieving life. Your style of existence revealed reality. Your tenderness, your honesty, your perspective. You knew how to live.

Now, gone from us, you still continue living, loving, laughing. For your Christmas present years ago, God healed you by taking you home. This season reminds me so much of you. You found so many ways of lifting us higher, of holding our hands, of hugging our necks, of taking us home. You were greater than any gift you wrapped.

That year? You battled each breath on this holiday.

This year? You celebrate every second in your holy home.

I miss you. One day I'll come for a visit that never ends. That Christmas there, I look forward to remembering.

Forever.

> *Your son,*
> *Christopher Maxwell*

The miraculous birth of The Baby makes possible the miraculous rebirth of a man and a woman.

—Dr. A. D. Beacham, Jr.

Reflection: Mary's Treasure

By Mary DeMent

But Mary treasured up all these things and pondered them in her heart.

— Luke 2:19

My hands hold your Holy Body
Me, Mary, the Hebrew girl next door
Holding a Holy God
God with us
God with me
God, please be with me
My heart has never beat faster
My head is full of reflection
Joseph comforts me with his touch
Father, please comfort him tonight
We've been through so much these past few months

What are people saying?
I wonder
Will they believe that this baby is from above? From You?
And, in fact, *is* You?

I can hardly believe it myself
It is all becoming quite real now though
Heavenly hosts surround us singing hallelujahs
Shepherds kneel and pay homage to this heaven come to earth
They too encountered angels visiting earth
Word is out that wise men are on their way as well
Bringing gifts no less
No less for a King
I'm holding a King
I'm holding THE King
I don't know if I am ready for all of this
The Savior of the world coming from my womb
I pray the world will see the family resemblance
When they see me, I pray they will see You
Emmanuel
God with us

> *Watch for this—a virgin will get pregnant*
> *and bear a son; They will name him Immanuel*
> *(Hebrew for "God is with us").*
>
> —Matthew 1:23, THE MESSAGE

Home: Jesus Here and Now

Then Jesus made a circuit of all the towns and villages. He taught in their meeting places, reported kingdom news, and healed their diseased bodies, healed their bruised and hurt lives. When he looked out over the crowds, his heart broke. So confused and aimless they were, like sheep with no shepherd. "What a huge harvest!" he said to his disciples. "How few workers! On your knees and pray for harvest hands!"

— Matthew 9:35–38 (THE MESSAGE)

Recently, my mind flooded with wild thoughts. What if Jesus came here? What if He came here today? No, I don't mean His second coming. I mean His first.

Suppose He was born in a homeless shelter in downtown Orlando. Since the stars are dimmed by the glare of city lights, the roar of jets lures 7-11 workers to visit His birthplace. Instead of leaving sheep on a hillside, they are drawn from the selling of beer.

His childhood days in a suburb receive no headlines or evening news. That changes, though, as He pulls around Him African-Americans, Hispanics, Caucasians and Native Americans from New York, Chicago, Phoenix, and even a couple of home boys.

Amazing surprises begin to happen.

What would my dreams wish for? Water into wine? No. I prefer fresh orange juice. Fish for a crowd? No. I'll let others wish for healthy seafood.

How about scrambled eggs, wheat toast, and sausage—all without cholesterol, of course? How about the price of gas going down? How about a little snow in Florida? Maybe a little more money and a few more friends. Maybe an MRI that tells me my brain has been healed. Maybe no more noisy neighbors and no more Christians deserting churches over picky issues. Sound okay?

I have a feeling that Christ's arrival in an entertainment environment would address ugly climates other than my petty preferences. In addition to parables about lizards, mosquitoes, swimming pools, mice, country music, bowl games, interest rates, tolls, and magic in the air, there would be more. Much more. Perhaps a visit to a well-known theme park to communicate with gays instead of casting votes in a church business meeting. He might avoid political debates, choosing, instead, to question the motives of major bureaucratic circles. He, no doubt, would spend little time watching religious TV, since that would rob His precious time away from ministering to the actors and actresses in violent, corrupt shows.

His years of training as a mechanic in His dad's business taught Him the importance of people struggles, so He might send His followers two-by-two to stand on the road, offering help to frightened drivers who need assistance at no charge. His E-mail debates with modern experts might cause His views to hit headlines. Critics might create massive Web sites for large audiences, winning people polls against the Strange Man who strolls through Orlando International Airport looking for ways to help others. He and His friends might eat at restaurants avoided by moral experts, then spend Sundays visiting prisoners at 33rd Street and give women a ride home in his old pickup truck.

Time spent? With AIDS patients, interracial couples, homeless children, counselors frazzled by overwork, preachers living alone after falling into sexual sins, the wives of such disappointments, a famous athlete kicked off his team because of drug addiction, lonely moms whose husbands love their vocations while missing vacations with the family, a beautiful teenage girl who avoids food just to lose a few more pounds, a liberal columnist who receives hate mail from those who call themselves God's people, a conservative broadcaster who really hates himself more than his opponents, and families going on vacations while the wide ride spins them into deeper debt.

Wouldn't He appear on church property? Sure. He would visit the alcoholic lottery player who lives alone in a broken-down bus behind a barn by a church's parking lot.

His home? Nursing homes, juvenile homes, mansions, shacks, hotels, homes destroyed by hurricanes and tornadoes, hidden homes in the inner city.

Well, He wasn't born here. My unique perspective presents intriguing events that will never happen.

Unless, of course, we let them happen through us.

> *The Son of God became a man to enable men to become the sons of God.*
>
> —C. S. Lewis

Chapter

12

Wounds: Sad Songs of the Season

And there were shepherds living out in the fields nearby, keeping watch over their flocks at night. An angel of the Lord appeared to them, and the glory of the Lord shone around them, and they were terrified. But the angel said to them, "Do not be afraid. I bring you good news of great joy that will be for all the people. Today in the town of David a Savior has been born to you; he is Christ the Lord. This will be a sign to you: You will find a baby wrapped in cloths and lying in a manger."

—Luke 2:8–12

Holiday sounds fill the air. Christmas carols, Yuletide tunes, the noise of joy and peace make the air thick with merriment.

Families and friends circle tables, hold hands, offer prayers, eat and laugh until full. Background music sets the mood. Presents and decorations dress the scene.

Not everyone is so happy. Not every song sings of smiles.

For the lonely, silent nights are too silent. Tinsel decks their hearts with grief; red and green blend to blue.

Where is money for the celebration? Where are friends for the sharing? For some, this Christmas is different. Painfully different.

Death came calling since last December. Now the house is too big, too empty.

Divorce came calling since last December. Now the children come here, go there. They come back then leave again. Whose turn is it?

Depression came calling since last December. Now the joy eludes, the peace hides.

Debt increases during this time of year. So does the suicide rate. Does caring? Does compassion?

Will our happy songs find a hearing among the sad this season? Will we make a difference for those with one less present under the tree this year? Is there a Present who lives on, who gives on, who sings a steady song of Good News?

Good news of great joy for ALL the people. So the angel sang.

All the people? All?

Not just the healthy, the wealthy, the handsome, the whole?

To the empty, the lonely, the sad, we can sing of news good and of joy great.

O, little towns and lonely hearts, lying still under a ceiling of silent stars, you sleep and wake deep and dreamless. But listen now. Hear this song I try my best to sing. Hear it. Maybe while listening, eyes can notice an everlasting light in dark streets shining. Maybe hopes and fears of this year will meet, will greet, will be handled.

In God's wondrous gift given, Baby born in Bethlehem. That is how.

I pray, singing. I plead, hoping.

Emmanuel, our Lord, come to us and to them; abide with us and them. In the happy and the sad, descend to us we pray. Come, we sing. We sing for all.

Change our tunes. Give us Yours.

Change our views. Gives us Yours.

For Christmas, give us You.

Christmas? The birth of hope and salvation. A time of celebration.

—Debbie Maxwell

Cleansing: God's Dreaming of a White Christmas

Suddenly a great company of the heavenly host appeared with the angel, praising God and saying,

"Glory to God in the highest, and on earth peace to men on whom his favor rests."

When the angels had left them and gone into heaven, the shepherds said to one another, "Let's go to Bethlehem and see this thing that has happened, which the Lord has told us about." So they hurried off and found Mary and Joseph, and the baby, who was lying in the manger.

— Luke 2:13–16

Common matches and marketing catches leave executives grinning. As they lowered hopes of seasonal sales success, grateful hearts result from money spent, deals lent, promises bent. For those whose businesses shiver, God's dreaming of a white Christmas.

Curious mix-ups and malfunctioning fix-ups leave multitudes confused. As eyes notice sins blocking light nearby and far away, grace longs to fall down the chimneys of humanistic methodology. For those willing to glance at His face, God's dreaming of a white Christmas.

Children list their wishes. And wait. Parents check their possibilities. And wait. Patients hope for better health. And wait. God's dreaming of a white Christmas.

If the story of a Baby is true maybe darkness can become light this year. If the story of a Baby is true, maybe smiles can cover faces this year. If the story of a Baby is true, maybe people feeling isolated can make friends this year; maybe people troubled by trials can feel a new breeze this year and maybe people worn weary by failures can notice the cleansing power of grace.

God? He's dreaming of a white Christmas. Not snow. Not ice. He dreams of a price paid to show lives changed. Joy on a Birthday Celebration.

Dream. With God, dream. He can bring a brightness and brilliance to us this year. Let us let Him climb down the chimneys of our habits, wake us from our passive sleep and shake us as He hands us the Gift of Grace with a smile on His face.

This December let us remember God's dream. Allow Him to wash us clean.

> *Christmas anticipation is about looking forward to Easter, because without Easter, Christmas has absolutely no meaning; so under all the Christmas carols ring the refrains of "Beneath the Cross of Jesus," "There is a Fountain Filled With Blood," and "When I Survey the Wondrous Cross" as I remember Jesus came at Christmas to die for me.*
>
> —Paul Smith

Together: The Then and Now

You are the light of the world. A city on a hill cannot be hidden. Neither do people light a lamp and put it under a bowl. Instead they put it on its stand, and it gives light to everyone in the house. In the same way, let your light shine before men, that they may see your good deeds and praise your Father in heaven.

— Matthew 5:14–16

When still living in Orlando, I remember my wife, three sons, and I visited Georgia during Thanksgiving. The air felt cooler there than our Orlando breeze back home. Friends and family smiled as we smiled. We ate together, filling ourselves with good food while telling great stories about the past and the present. Both of those, the then and the now, can teach us so much.

Clocks continue ticking. Children keep growing up. The earth rotates regularly while birthdays add ages and bodies wear out. Newspapers place almanacs and obituaries near wedding announcements, real estate deals, school lunches, games stats, and names of newborn babies. The old and the new. The coming and the going. The then and the now.

I remember much about my twenty-two years in north Georgia. I visit Elberton, grateful that my family built a solid foundation of life. My elementary school is gone now. Tate Street seems smaller now. Still, the Granite Capital remains stabile and consistent. Routines can maintain stone beliefs in a world where wavering and wandering appear as the norm.

I visit Royston, remembering that heroes can come from anywhere, that cancer took my mother's body but not her spirit, that teen years teach us so much, and that we can lead while learning and laugh while crying. I visit Franklin Springs, rejoicing that Living Water does flow on and on and on. Wars and debates and disagreements and turmoil cannot defeat the steady stream of Truth that others spilled into this young man. I visit Athens, realizing that their Dawgs usually defeat my Jackets and life still goes on. I visit Atlanta, remembering taking Mama for chemotherapy and realizing these bodies don't last forever.

I didn't know I would live there again and enjoy Christmas in the towns of my youth.

In those younger days I watched Braves games when they lost during the season and never had a chance to lose during the playoffs. Being a child playing football in the Granite Bowl and a teen playing basketball for Franklin County seems so long ago. When I traveled there for holiday moments with family, I peeked back. The places looked so different. And so much the same.

While there for that Christmas visit, my sons hit balls over the fence where I hit my only career homer. Is the field smaller? Now, my big mansion on Tate Street has shrunk. My house in Springdale has aged. I saw housing developments where I once walked alone in the woods, where I previously saw deer and rabbits, where I formerly raced through the woods on my motorcycle.

So different. So much the same.

We mingle tradition with recent. We merge the ancient with the modern. Slowly cooked meats sit on a table beside microwaved food. The elderly, who love the way things used to be, also love how today's technology allows them to hear again, see again, and breath while holding portable phones to talk to a grandchild through Skype around the world.

Yes, before Web sites and chat rooms, holidays still came. Before contemporary praise songs on PowerPoint presentations, congregations held hymnals. But before those holy hymns, Charles Wesley heard a Voice instructing him that the modern melodies of his culture were okay to use on Sundays. It doesn't offend Mr. Wesley when I tell him I had trouble understanding a few of those hymns in my early Methodist days or that I love hearing my sons sing David's songs—didn't they come earlier than hymns, the King James version, and football bowl games?—in a style blending truth (then) within their grasp (now).

Yes, before the Varsity added improved restrooms, those chili dawgs tasted better than any other I've located. They still do. But, honestly, I like new and improved facilities when the food just might motivate a trip toward that modernized room.

I'm pleased we no longer need outhouses. I like airplanes, fresh paint, fresh food, and fresh ways to say Ancient Truth. Though my 1,131 mile journeys to places of my past tricked me a few times with unknown bypasses here and there, I'm glad I'm not determined to pass by the "now" just to live in the "then." I can still drive through a town I hope to see. I can also drive around if that is best for me.

History plus the present can offer us a gift that allows my story, your story, and an old, old story about a Baby's birth to become more real this December.

And maybe, we might move back into a town of our past and smile as we remember the stories.

Christmas is the day Jesus left His place to come live at my place, so someday soon I can leave my place and go live at His place.

—Ann Floyd

Chapter 15

Favored: I Wish You a *Mary* Christmas

By Mary DeMent

S he tired easily these days. She was not prepared for the emotional and physical roller coaster of the past few months. At first, it seemed she was exhausted all the time. Next, she experienced a burst of energy. Then the cycle repeated itself. She was forgetful and prone to accidents. She found herself crying for no apparent reason. She became annoyed over things that never used to bother her. Initially, nothing tasted good. The very sight of food nauseated her. Now, everything she tasted was full of flavor.

As the time drew near, she cleaned and prepared her "nest" for their new arrival. She made the necessary arrangements to welcome this new child God promised, the Promised Child of God. Her plans were all coming together.

Then, Caesar Augustus issued a decree that a census be taken. Everyone needed to return to his or her hometown to register. So Mary, very much "with child," left Nazareth together with Joseph, her betrothed, to register in the town of Bethlehem. "While they were there, the time came for the baby to be born, and she gave birth to her firstborn, a son. She wrapped him in cloths and placed him in a manger because there was no room for them in the inn" (Luke 2:6, 7).

I've been thinking a lot about Mary lately. Not only do I share her name, but I've shared her "condition" four times. I remember pregnancy all too well.

Pregnancy is an exciting time. It's an adventure. But I can't say I'd be willing to leave home (nor would my doctor allow it) given the overwhelming possibility that I'd give birth "on the road." I think that may be the very reason God chose Mary to carry His One and Only. She was willing to be obedient. As she arranged to leave for Bethlehem, surely Mary knew she would deliver her baby away from the comfort of her self-prepared nest.

Yet Scripture shows no record of any hesitation. Mary just did what was required of her by her leader. "Nesting" is a very powerful urge to have everything ready for the arrival of your baby. Mary left all her preparations and plans behind in Nazareth. Then she bore her Child in a barn and laid Him down on that authentic nesting material—straw.

Some have chosen to place Mary above Jesus. She does not belong there. But, let's not dismiss her position either. Remember what the angel told her? "Greetings, you who are highly favored! The Lord is with you" (Luke 1:28). Mary: highly favored by God, blessed among women.

I want to become more like that Mary: obedient, willing to go, to stay, to remain in God's hands. I wish you all a "Mary" Christmas this season. Plans shift; emotions fluctuate. Let's align ourselves with God's plan. And, let's embrace Mary's attitude: "I am the Lord's servant," Mary answered, "May it be to me as you have said." (Luke 1:38).

She gave birth to a son, her firstborn. She wrapped him in a blanket and laid him in a manger, because there was no room in the hostel.

—Luke 2:7, THE MESSAGE

Chapter 16

Nearby: A Modern Virgin in an Ancient Story

When Joseph woke up, he did what the angel of the Lord had commanded him and took Mary home as his wife. But he had no union with her until she gave birth to a son. And he gave him the name Jesus.

— Matthew 1:24, 25

1. Maria's Pregnant! Where's the Father?

Maria likes autumn. Especially since summers in central Florida bring too much heat for her in a home without air conditioning. A little bit of coolness could help. Usually, she feels so relaxed, so young, so refreshed this time of year.

Those pleasant hopes of a few peaceful moments have long departed on this occasion. Pain arrived when Maria became pregnant.

Hurts appeared as family and friends doubted her, as they humiliated this frightened fifteen-year-old. Humor once held a place in her heart. Now, tired and heavy, feeling a child inside moving and growing, she endures almost alone.

Her father departed long ago. Living with her mother and grandmother, they lost their first home when Orlando's big city plans needed more room. An arena, a new business venture, a downtown tower. Now, Maria, Mama, and Abuela live in a three-room house: a kitchen for cooking and eating, a bedroom for the whole family, a restroom. Relatives arrive, stay nights, then leave with little warning.

Many of her friends have been pregnant at her age. Some, even younger. They saw no disadvantage when she announced her future.

The problem came when she claimed to have never made love to a man. All of them laughed, assuming her joke would quickly end when she realized her condition fit the norm. Several suggested abortion. Others accused her of making up the story because she had slept with so many men she simply did not know the father's name.

Her cousin, a denominational bishop and powerful speaker, informed Maria—the one who had been his favorite relative—that things would never be the same. She was not sure what he meant. When he avoided her after that, she learned the point of his sermon. Rejection. And it came from him.

An uncle always enjoyed his time with Maria. She misses him since he went to prison. His drinks and drugs drove him there. She thought of him because she felt he would accept her. She would never know for sure.

Maria weeps often. Especially about José. Older, but strong and kind, her boyfriend really cares for her. Until now he also doubted, questioning and denying her conclusions. He knew he was not the father. He also knew someone had to be. She wondered if he would ever know for sure. Maria loved life when he learned the truth.

Yesterday the pregnant young female saw her friend. José smiled, his first grin in months. She knew then that he knew.

Would anyone else ever learn and believe? Would the impossible news of pregnancy without an understandable explanation ever bring smiles of joy instead of ridicule? How long would questions live without answers? Will this life emerge like a death?

Maria and José listen to traffic, to a train. They hear a siren. Home tomorrow is unknown today. For this moment in time they know their Child and their God care for them. Right here and right now, in the middle of a city that has little room except for sin.

She feels the Baby move.

2. Eight Months and Counting

Time continues. Maria, eight months pregnant, knows a time will quickly arrive when lives will change. Many lives? Change forever? Yes, in the present tension, that time begins. Decisions frightened her before, but now when she should feel the most afraid, she feels thrilled.

Many still make fun of her. Who can blame them? She fits the role in age, actions, conditions, decisions. Except for one, really. By claiming belief in the lack of involvement necessary to place her in that present situation, she maintains something too impossible to blend with the standards.

Orange Blossom Trail has a reputation for crime, poverty, prostitution, and X-rated movies. What many people pay to see is what many people are willing to pay to get.

Though local leaders have attempted to improve the area, the enriched appearance does not change its history. Problems still surround this world within a world. The lives of people who do not fit the scales of massive acceptance fill that well-known street. South of Orlando and right at home for hopelessness: that's the neighborhood they know.

Maria grew up in that environment. Prostitution earns a living for her friends. For many, it provides money while drugs and alcohol spend the dollars quickly in a family heritage of hurt and uncertainty. Maria was surrounded by those who fit that norm. Some thought she would. Some think she does. Especially now.

One friend treats Maria better now than ever. Her kindness does not hide her hopes: she sees Maria as an opportunity to draw in a sales rep. José can make very little money from his present hourly labor. If he worked for Maria's friend selling drugs, his income could take a giant leap. Comparing a quick twenty to his $5.65 per hour reveals much. But the hopes from José's heart reach different conclusions.

Slowly walking south today, Maria hears giggles from mouths near the eyes that watch her struggle. Step by step, a life within, an unknown future, physical struggles, mental uncertainties. Her mind still blends her heritage and her present condition as an amazing miracle. Maria does not complain. She stays sane. She breathes.

Rejected by the wealthy because of her poverty, ridiculed by friends because she claims virginity, this little girl gives thanks to a God she gladly blames for her plight. She believes, really believes, that her God planted the seed within her, that He will honor the promise sent by an angel. Maria often reminds herself of those words she says she heard: "The Lord is with you. You have found favor. Have no fear." Blending the honesty of blues with the joy of her hopes, she sings to celebrate and prompt her memories. Maria is pleased at the great things of her God.

José and Maria meet for a Thanksgiving dinner with family. The little food and few friends: that is enough. For now. The future offers hope.

Worry stops. They say a prayer, asking for blessings. Eating starts. José, intermingling a mix of faith and fear, enjoys these moments. He smiles.

Maria eats with hopes that her son is pleased.

Many days await, and many lives await, to live with hopes that her Son is pleased.

3. Glorious Day! The Baby's Born!

Hotels in the dark, drug-welcomed world of downtown Orlando expect the worst. They can fill quickly, close briefly, then open again for new people needing food or longing for affection.

Most rooms shift by the hour. Many become homes for those who have nowhere else to go. Or, those who want nowhere else to attempt to go.

As Maria and José walk slowly through the cool Central Florida evening, they want and need a place to stop. No one offered to drive them to the hospital. No insurance company will cover the cost. So they journey through the world they know, the world that knows them, the world that knows them not.

Voices shout from the corner woods near The Citrus Bowl. Traffic races.

Covered by trees, housing developments hide without walls. Location itself lumps it under the alone region. No buildings. Many bushes. Night by night, people sleep just off the streets. They seem to know each other. No family, few friends, no jobs. They long for a little food to eat, for too much to drink, for a few smiles to seem real. None of them expected the events of this night.

Maybe Maria and José and a Baby Boy would somehow change things.

They continue walking. Slowly. Time passes. Her body hurts, feeling that passage of time.

The delay ends. Maria informs José that now is the time and this, that dark world of nothing and nobody, that lonely home of helplessness, must be the room for a Child to be born.

Maria stops, sits and begins to release the mystery. She hurts, closes her eyes. She smiles. She knows. A Son arrives and cries. His voice makes noise. He cried, while seeming to sing alone. More, many more, sounds of joy cover the downtown world with celebration.

Voices with power and praise. From where? Who offers those cheers with such pleasure?

Bright lights push away darkness and cover the world Maria and José know, the world they now see as new, as brand new, as good, as glorious.

Heaven enters this home. Angels, with melodies of peace and delight, mention the message of a Baby born. A Son has arrived.

The Father they sing about is the Father for whom and to whom they sing. Their Owner and Maker. They sing to Him today.

He is pleased with the sound He hears.

He is pleased with the Son He sees.

He knows His plan: offering the Life of Himself to offer a never-ending life for all who believe.

Maria clings to her newborn as she now begins to relax. She wonders: Wouldn't it be wonderful to celebrate His birthday every year?

Instead of people enjoying a holiday by spending too much money for a reminder of riches and wishes, what if the world celebrated the birthday of Maria's Son? What if His life brought such a gift that the planet joined in, singing with the shining choir of heaven?

Maria wonders. Her Baby cries. She holds Him tightly, feeling He would one day hold her.

The homeless people move in close. They stare but stay silent. They see her Son.

Finally, after so many years, they feel right at home.

On that holy night God penetrated our existence with life.

—Curt Dalaba

Recreated: A World with Ears to Hear

*So Joseph also went up from the town of Naza-
reth in Galilee to Judea, to Bethlehem the town of
David, because he belonged to the house and line of
David. He went there to register with Mary, who was
pledged to be married to him and was expecting a
child. While they were there, the time came for the
baby to be born, and she gave birth to her firstborn,
a son. She wrapped him in cloths and placed him in
a manger, because there was no room for them in
the inn.*

— Luke 2:4–7

A Baby cried; the silence died.

The Boy grew: an Alive World sounded louder, filling the vacuum of silent centuries.

A mother, so young, carried Him, held Him. She listened and loved the growing Voice of God.

An old man, bent and crippled for years by bearing the burdens of his fears, deaf and dumb from decades of hearing and saying nothing, heard the Word. His eyes opened; his back straightened. The Word became his friend. The old man learned from his young Tutor. Soon, the man spoke and sounded strangely like his Teacher.

A priest knew the rules and requirements, and met them proudly. He spoke words. Often and in public, he spoke many words. Old words. Dead words. Words added by man, the addendum to a complete, solid-as-stone word given long before. Stories from the Alive Word flew to the ears of that priest who continued reciting his prayers. The priest could not hear God above his own voice.

A lonely woman had heard the words of many men—men who assured her of their love as they assigned her duties. She performed, they paid; that was the love she heard of. But this, this was so new: God's Voice talked to her, talked of giving instead of taking, of choices instead of chores. His words and His tone, His expressions and His explanations sounded like an invitation rather than condemnation. She loved the Word who loved her. She learned the words and lived again, loving a world with them.

A religion collected dust. No sound waves blew across the kept canon. No challenges. No changes. Neat and quiet, the noiseless liturgy disturbed no one. Then, the Word spoke abruptly, shattering the stained-glass cage. Dust flew, but few knew how thick it had grown.

Deep silence dies slowly, if at all.

A place waited. It now felt recreated. The planet danced: an awed world hearing love, finding a Voice of sure celebration.

Joy to the world. To young mothers and bent old men, to lonely women and all who have ears to hear: joy to the world.

The Word is come. Let earth receive His Voice.

> *The Gift of God, wrapped in flesh and baby blankets, still causes angels and wise men and shepherds and me to sing with joy and worship in awe, today!*

> —Terry Raburn

Chapter
18

Celebrate: The Most Wonderful Time

By Mary DeMent

I peer through the display and grin at the clerk. "Here we go again," I offer. She smiles and manages a sigh. Christmas is just around the corner. And no one knows how to celebrate quite like American retailers! On November 1st, plastic pumpkins and costumes make their way to the discount shelf. A dazzling array of reds and greens bid them farewell. Stacks of boxes line the aisles, preparing the way for the Christ child.

I know many despise the commercialization of Christmas. But, I find myself welcoming the madness! I take pleasure in the browsing and the buying. There are so many nice things. I want to pick up every one. I hold them and think of who would appreciate the present. I love the way some stores arrange gift baskets donned with ribbons and bows. I enjoy the bright lights and the sounds of the season. It *is* the "most wonderful time of the year!"

Some may caution, "Careful Mary, you're getting caught up in the season and forgetting the reason." But to them I say, "Nonsense! Join me!" Give yourself over to the lights, the smells, the sounds and even the hustle and the bustle. Send cards and sing songs. Bake bread and cookies. Put money in the kettle. Put tinsel on the tree. Get caught up! "It's the most wonderful time of the year!"

Approach the season with excitement! The birth of Christ! He *is* Emmanuel. Think about it. Talk about it! God *with* us! Celebrate His birth! Celebrate His life! Celebrate the season! For the season reminds us, reminds *all* mankind of the birth of Jesus Christ, Our Lord!

Don't allow Christmas to break your bank account. But, do allow it to break you out of your normal routine. Oh, you don't have much of a choice, do you? Longer lines, heavy traffic, holiday happenings. You may wish to escape it all. I challenge you to embrace it! Embrace the season. Embrace the reason. And, relax. Really, relax. Allow the Joy of the Lord to be your strength!

For unto you is born this day in the city of David a Saviour, which is Christ the Lord. And this shall be a sign unto you; Ye shall find the babe wrapped in swaddling clothes, lying in a manger. And suddenly there was with the angel a multitude of the heavenly host praising God, and saying, Glory to God in the highest, and on earth peace, good will toward men (Luke 2:11–14, KJV).

Peace and goodwill to you during this most wonderful time of the year.

> *Christmas is one time the world gets to glory in the message without being religious.*
>
> —John Fischer

Requests: Asking for Presents

No longer will a man teach his neighbor,
or a man his brother, saying, "Know the LORD,"
because they will all know me,
from the least of them to the greatest,
declares the LORD.
"For I will forgive their wickedness
and will remember their sins no more."

— Jeremiah 31:34

The old song confessed, "All I want for Christmas is my two front teeth." I heard it. Even sang it. Never really asked for that gift of two teeth, though. I might later. As of today, my list does not include that request.

What do I want? On December 25, as wars and rumors of wars continue, as sickness and sadness merge decorations and celebrations, as envy invades hearts of those who ignore blessings, what do I really want?

Glad you asked. Actually, I'm glad the Giver instructs me to ask Him for a confession of my hopes, dreams, and desires. He sits, covered in holiness, listening to the requests of little-boy-Chris at Christmas.

Here are my rhyming wishes:

1. Pray.

My most frequent petition must hit the top of my holiday wish list. I pray for prayer. I write and speak about it, dreaming we will march with David, plead with Paul, and intercede like Hyde or Murray or Eastman. I ask the Listener to motivate, encourage, challenge, and compel us to pray more often. For His birthday, I ask for prayer.

2. Stay.

In a world of comers and goers, the emotionally addicted seek a sudden cure for any ailment. The word "shifts" doesn't refer to hours worked, but to twists and turns from one career or commitment or concern to another that promises more sure, or more sensual, or more sudden satisfaction. Stability, traded in search of quick fixes, finds little room available in the modern inn of hurry. For His birthday, I pray to stay.

3. Pay.

I think of my years pastoring. We avoided the non-stop pleading for monetary feasts. We chose to never echo the television trend of prophecies that promise those who give to them will always get something back. We decided to stir biblical truth about finances with all Scripture, not just with shoves and pushes until payments arrive. Countless people need money to come before this year concludes. For His birthday, I follow God's instructions and ask for a miracle of money for many.

4. Say.

We talk. Often. Weather, sports, music, politics. At restaurants. On phones. Through E-mail. In offices. Using Twitter and Facebook and texting. But I dream of a willingness within us to announce the Greatest Gift of All to those who need Him. Debate about doctrinal beliefs only truly matters to God if He matters enough to us that we pass Him around to others. For His birthday, I hope to say words of truth—handing Him, that Presence, to someone waiting and watching.

Four requests. For others, for me, for us, for all. Though from Him, actually for Him.

Asking does not offend the Provider of Presents.

Refusing to ask does.

Kneel nearby. Cry out your requests. Then meet the Sacred King as He drops in, deciding to be home with us for Christmas.

> *He who has not Christmas in his heart will never find it under a tree.*
>
> —Roy L. Smith

Chapter 20

Hope: 'Tis the Season

Remembrance, like a candle, burns brightest
at Christmastime.

—Charles Dickens[7]

'Tis the season to be jolly. So the song says. Joining with commercials and colors come the smiles and meals and families and fun. They all find time on the table. On all tables?

'Tis the season to be sad. Commercialism colors scenes in ways that beg us to do more than we should. Too much. Too few. Blessings, or so they appear, become curses passed through. Money? The dreams delete resources saved for needs and toss them to wants. Memories? Maybe the way-back-whens weigh too heavily upon us. Alone? Many of us have family and friends while many others long for either.

Suicide? Why do the rates rise on this occasion of Hope given?

'Tis the season to see Jesus. A Baby King born at such an unexpected place. A Body Crucified to take my place. From manger sights to darkened nights, from miracles performed to blood dripping, from doves of blessings to a death on a tree. Jesus is the One I must see. Today. Tomorrow. Christmas Eve. Christmas Day. Everyday in a brand new year: That is the season.

'Tis the season to be accepted. If I see Him, if I realize how He really sees me, maybe I can find room at the inn. The inner inn, the real world of life, of Life. Maybe it is the time to take John at his words about a Word given, a Word to be taken, for a world that includes room for us to be shaken:

"For God so loved the world, that he gave his one and only Son, that whoever believes in him shall not perish but have eternal life" (John 3:16).

So if a Christian is touched only once a year, the touching is still worth it, and maybe on some given Christmas, some quiet morning, the touch will take.

—Harry Reasoner[8]

79

Chapter
21

Priceless: Wrapped
and Waiting

By Mary DeMent

As a child, I made gifts to give away at Christmas. Since my Dad was a carpenter, there were always plenty of resources at my fingertips.

One year, I created a multi-level plant stand for my Aunt Janet and Uncle Charles. The stand was huge! There were three shelves at the bottom, two in the middle and one on top. Attempting to wrap the odd-shaped gift proved a real feat. I believe I resorted to using newspaper and a lot of tape. It wasn't the best wrap job, but as the cliché goes, "it's the thought that counts." I sure hoped they would not form an opinion of my gift by the wrapping.

We tend to think that the best gifts are those that "look" the nicest. Ribbons and bows are appealing to the eye. We imagine the bigger the better. That is not always true though. Sometimes treasures are found wrapped up in the simple things of life: a smile, the laughter of children, a stroll on the beach. A shiny, new car may fill a void in your life for a season. But the smile and acceptance of a new friend could fill your life with joy all year long. A new toy offers momentary satisfaction, but time spent with Mom or Dad at the park is priceless.

This time of year we concentrate upon another gift. This gift, like mine, was not draped in the finest of wrappings. Jesus, we read, was "wrapped in cloths" (Luke 2:7). And considering the socioeconomic status of Mary and Joseph, they probably were not premium cloths. Think about it: the Savior of the world, the greatest Christmas gift of all, was wrapped in everyday linen.

> *Joy to the world, the Lord has come. Let earth receive her King. Let every heart prepare Him room.*

My uncle retired from the United States Air Force several years ago. Their home contained exceptional trinkets and gifts from their travels around the world. During a visit to their home in Edison, Georgia, before their deaths, I spied a familiar piece. However, this piece wasn't from Morocco, Turkey, or any other foreign soil. No, there among their cultural treasures, stood a rickety old plant stand. I was honored to learn that they had made room for the piece all these years.

Receive the King this Christmas. Receive Him for the first time or receive Him anew. But make room for Him. Make room for this royalty who came in rags. Keep Him at the center of your home, your heart for years to come. A relationship with Emmanuel, God with us, is the finest treasure you will find.

> *Love came down at Christmas;*
> *Love all lovely, love divine;*
> *Love was born at Christmas,*
> *Stars and angels gave the sign.*

—Christina Rossetti[9]

Chapter

22

Purpose: A Summary of Success

When they had seen him, they spread the word concerning what had been told them about this child, and all who heard it were amazed at what the shepherds said to them. But Mary treasured up all these things and pondered them in her heart. The shepherds returned, glorifying and praising God for all the things they had heard and seen, which were just as they had been told.

Now there was a man in Jerusalem called Simeon, who was righteous and devout. He was waiting for the consolation of Israel, and the Holy Spirit was upon him. It had been revealed to him by the Holy Spirit that he would not die before he had seen the Lord's Christ. Moved by the Spirit, he went into the temple courts. When the parents brought in the child Jesus to do for him what the custom of the Law required, Simeon took him in his arms and praised God, saying: "Sovereign Lord, as you have promised, you now dismiss your servant in peace. For my eyes have seen your salvation, which you have prepared in the sight of all people, a light for revelation to the Gentiles and for glory to your people Israel."

Luke 2:17–20, 25–32

Let's simplify it. Instead of declaring doctrinal terminology or defining unexplainable beliefs, let's narrow our wide range of theology. One of our friends did the same thing.

He knew the skills of communication. Confrontations and illustrations and explanations. Stories and Scriptures and symbolism. To crowds, to disciples, to prostitutes. Money, miracles, masses. That Friend applied a wide range of teaching truth to His audience.

So, how did He simplify and narrow the large formula for successful faith? How could He supply a summary of commandments, laws, warnings, and promises? How did He respond to a listener's question after debating dialogue with religious leaders about dollars on earth and marriage in heaven?

"If you love God completely and love others like you love yourself," Jesus said, "You've got it."

He said nothing was greater than that. He still says nothing is greater than that. Jesus glanced at 10 Commandments, 613 Laws, 39 books of history, philosophy, poetry, prayer and prophecy. Mixed in what we call the Old Testament, He downloaded it into one file with two menus. Love God. Love people. Not feelings or romance, pleasure or gratification, self-seeking or self-promoting. In attitudes, in actions: love Him and them.

Let's picture Jesus beside us. Don't ask for the I'm-in-a-hurry-so-preach-quick version of truth. We already know His response. Ask this: "Jesus, how do I rate in loving God, myself and others?"

What would He say on a day like today?

And all the way, men everywhere were whispering
that the long-awaited Troubadour had come.
"It is he," they said, "at last he's come. Praise the
Father–Spirit, he has come."

—Calvin Miller, *The Singer*[10]

Chapter 23

Authenticity: Inside Matters

Therefore the Lord himself will give you a sign: The
virgin will be with child and will give birth to a son,
and will call him Immanuel.

— Isaiah 7:14

t he paper protected the present.
it also presented the gift as something
it wasn't.
colors, images.
a cover, a mask.
though lovely and friendly,
the imagery lies about reality.
paper, protecting and promoting
a fictional fix
cast in a mix
of amazement,
does its task of deception.

is it something i want,
or something i wait for?
is it someone i am,
or someone i long to become?

don't the gifts give way
on a holiday?
aren't they torn opened to trash the covers aside?
they are
because what is inside matters.

what paper protects our presence?
why do i pretend, presenting me as someone
i'm not?
i must remove
the colors, images.
i must rip
my cover, my mask.
i'll give the Worker the task
of tearing, opening, trashing
that old me away,
and convincing me
this Christmas:
what is inside is
what matters.

*At Christmas we celebrate the in-the-flesh birth
that made possible our "in the Spirit rebirth."*

—Douglas B. Barton

Chapter
24

Compassion: A Month for Love

Therefore, if you are offering your gift at the altar and there remember that your brother has something against you, leave your gift there in front of the altar. First go and be reconciled to your brother; then come and offer your gift.

— Matthew 5:23, 24

February reminds us of romance. Songs, commercials, and cards inform us of the duties and delights we label as love. Valentine's Day gifts go on sale right after Christmas.

Let's not wait until January for a resolution or February for love. Let's begin today.

This time, we'll leave off the songs, the scenes, the stories. Instead, here is a Love List. Glance at the assignment. See possibilities for acts of kindness. Choose to live in love, replacing missed opportunities with ministry moments.

- Smile at a friend. Thank them for the many blessings they bring your way.
- Smile at a stranger. A glance from eyes of one displaying God's love is such a contrast to the common looks of lust or anger.
- Forgive someone who hurt you. Realize how the Loving God has forgiven you.
- Write a note. Make a call. Send a check.
- Serve a meal.
- Engage in conversation as the one listening.
- Do to others as you wish others would do to you.
- Do something for someone who has been kind to you.
- Do something for someone who has done wrong to you.
- Verbally thank someone who has cared for you, confronted you, corrected you, cautioned you, and continued to love you despite your mistakes.

- Pray for someone. Keep it between you and God. Believe He will bless them in amazing ways.
- Refuse to let a problem about another person stay with you in this year. Love enough to really, really, really forgive.

Resentment, bitterness, and a lack of forgiveness anchor us to a past that cannot be changed. We cannot go back and undo the damage of yesterday, but we can undo the damage it is causing us today. We do that with the act of forgiveness.

—Stephen Arterburn: *Healing is a Choice*

Chapter 25

Request: Asking Again

The child's father and mother marveled at what was said about him. Then Simeon blessed them and said to Mary, his mother: "This child is destined to cause the falling and rising of many in Israel, and to be a sign that will be spoken against, so that the thoughts of many hearts will be revealed. And a sword will pierce your own soul too."

When Joseph and Mary had done everything required by the Law of the Lord, they returned to Galilee to their own town of Nazareth. And the child grew and became strong; he was filled with wisdom, and the grace of God was upon him.

—Luke 2:33–35, 39, 40

I 'm still asking for the same gift. Has that ever happened to you?

Maybe you received what you wanted and liked it so much you decided to request another one. Maybe you lost the first gift and wanted a new one just like it. Maybe you had given the first away to a friend and still miss having it. Maybe you asked for it and the requested gift never arrived.

Whatever the reason, sometimes we ask again and again for the same gift.

Since it is December and a reminder of Christ's birth, it fits to talk about gifts. Since God gave the greatest gift of all and loves to continue giving, it suits Him for me to write about gifts.

December also concludes another year. So I looked back to my prayer theme for 2004. And, in the closing weeks and days of this year, I repeat my prayer from that year. I'm still asking God for the same gift.

What was my request for the year? As I studied Luke's historical report of Jesus changing the world, I wanted the description of Christ's early days to summarize my own growth:

> *And the child grew and became strong; he was filled with wisdom, and the grace of God was upon him.*
> (Luke 2:40)

Congregations sing and celebrate the Baby Jesus in December. While instructed to remember His life, during this month we focus more on the shepherds and angels, Mary and Joseph, stars and a Child.

The Child did not stay little. He, as the text informs us, grew. Growing, He became strong. Becoming strong, He was filled with wisdom. And, covering each element of His life, the grace of God was upon Him.

That was my prayer for 2004. I made it personal, asking for God to help me, my family, my friends, and my congregation to grow, become strong, and be filled with wisdom. I asked that His grace would be upon us.

As this December hits us, I'm still praying that same prayer. Again and again, God has heard me. Again and again, I believe He has answered in a variety of ways. And today, I pray it again.

What can you offer for Christmas? Join me in praying that prayer. Ask for growth and strength, for wisdom and grace.

Ask it again. Then let us be ready for what might happen to us.

> *My gracious Redeemer, My Savior art Thou.*
> *If ever I loved Thee, My Jesus, 'tis now.*
>
> —William R. Featherston,
> *My Jesus, I Love Thee*

Conclusion

A Departure, An Arrival

On reaching Jerusalem, Jesus entered the temple area and began driving out those who were buying and selling there. He overturned the tables of the moneychangers and the benches of those selling doves, and would not allow anyone to carry merchandise through the temple courts. And as he taught them, he said, "Is it not written: "'My house will be called a house of prayer for all nations'? But you have made it 'a den of robbers.'"

The chief priests and the teachers of the law heard this and began looking for a way to kill him, for they feared him, because the whole crowd was amazed at his teaching.

When evening came, they went out of the city.

— Mark 11:15–19

nother day and another year. An end, a finish. A start, a dawn. A closing and an opening. A reminder of the rapid pace of time. A revelation of the rushing water's flow.

We cannot slow time. We cannot stop it or control it.

What can we do? We can end this year as we should: analyzing the year ending, repenting of wrong, renewing our commitments, receiving Help, and listing our dreams of a year arriving.

Enough written by me.

Read the Instruction Manual covered with history, prayers, songs, opportunities and warnings. This best seller is the Best Teller of truth available. End a year and begin a year with Hope.

No excuses.

> *Our moods may shift, but God's doesn't. Our minds may change, but God's doesn't. Our devotion may falter, but God's never does.*
>
> —Max Lucado, *Traveling Light*

Endnotes

1. http://www.quotegarden.com/christmas.html (Accessed July 28, 2010)

2. Henry Van Dyke, *The Spirit of Christmas* (New York: Charles Scribner's Sons, 1905), 46–48.

3. http://www.quotegarden.com/christmas.html (Accessed July 22, 2010)

4. http://www.quotelady.com/subjects/christmas.html (Accessed July 22, 2010)

5. *"Communicating the Word in a Changing Society: That Glorious Song of Old"* Issachar File, December 1999.

6. Ibid

7. http://www.all-famous-quotes.com/religious_christmas_quotes.html (Accessed July 24, 2010.)

8. http://halife.com/speakers/christmasquotes.html (Accessed July 24, 2010)

9. http://www.quotelady.com/subjects/christmas.html (Accessed August 27, 2010)

10. Calvin Miller, *The Singer* (Downers Grove, IL: InterVarsity Press, 1975), 52.

About Chris Maxwell

Chris Maxwell grew up in northeast Georgia. After graduating from Emmanuel College, Chris and his wife Debbie moved to Orlando, Florida. They lived there 24 years where Debbie taught school and Chris served five years as a youth pastor and 19 years as a lead pastor. During that time they enjoyed watching their three sons, Taylor, Aaron, and Graham grow up quickly. In addition to loving God, sports, music, and books, Chris has always loved writing.

He has written articles, curriculum, devotionals, columns, reviews, and commercials for many companies. His book *Beggars Can Be Chosen* studies the stories of Christ's invitations, and his book *Changing My Mind* is the honest journal of his near death experience with encephalitis.

Chris now lives with epilepsy, and travels around the world to tell his story and interview others who have similar stories of life-changing experiences. Chris and Debbie moved back to Georgia in 2006 where Chris serves as Campus Pastor and Director of Spiritual Life at Emmanuel College and Debbie teaches fifth grade in an area elementary school. Taylor and his wife Brittany have a son, Anthem.

Connect With Chris...

For more information on Chris, read his blog, *Another Day Along the Way*, join the Facebook Chris Maxwell Readers Group, and visit his Web site, at **www.chrismaxwellweb.com**.

Additional Books by Chris Maxwell

Changing My Mind: A Journey of Disability and Joy
http://chrismaxwellweb.com/books/changing-my-mind

In *Changing My Mind*, Maxwell's creative narrative welcomes others into his battle with encephalitis and the resulting epilepsy. His honest journal reveals a damaged brain and life changes, inviting readers to face their own inner wars, their painful struggles, their disabilities, and to believe a Listener can turn their mourning into dancing.

Changing My Mind gives victims, their family members and friends, a better glance of true joy during journeys through the valleys, the shadows of death, the disappointments and the victories.

Beggars Can Be Chosen: In Spiritual Journey Through the Invitations of Jesus

http://chrismaxwellweb.com/books/beggars-can-be-chosen

About this book Chris explains, "My prayer is that by entering these stories we will allow Jesus to challenge our customs and clichés, enabling us to forge a new, more biblical style of evangelism."

Beggars Can Be Chosen probes the encounters of Christ and those He invited to follow Him. It is a book for those who have accepted His invitation and for those who are searching for answers to some of life's most probing questions.

There is a dual objective in *Beggars Can Be Chosen*: How is Jesus inviting us to follow Him? How does Jesus invite others to Himself through us?

Traveling chronologically through the life of Christ, the text takes the reader on a stirring journey. The stories vary in pace and emphasis, but the focus stays true to the objective.

Most Christians know evangelism is a must. We often try and fail. We live plagued by the nagging guilt of ineffectiveness. Beggars Can Be Chosen reveals how the Great Commission flowed naturally through Christ's life. People are tired of programs. This book presents the Person of Jesus as the true method of evangelism.

Beggars Can Be Chosen draws from a wealth of classic and contemporary sources of insight and information. Anecdotes, textual explanations, and stinging discourse provide moving meditations. Examples of ministries following Christ's example are displayed. Readers will know they have turned their attention to the Master Inviter.

To purchase either of Chris' books, please visit www. chrismaxwellweb.com or www.amazon.com.

About Mary DeMent

Mary DeMent is a freelance writer and web content manager. She lives in Orlando, Florida, with her husband Bill and their four children: Zane, Lauren, Samuel, and David.

She holds a Master's Degree in Clinical Social Work from the University of Central Florida and writes devotionals and articles for God's Word For Today, LIVE!, Next Generation Institute, and Faith Café.

Connect With Mary...

Many enjoy reading Mary's blog, *Life Matters*, at **www.marydement.blogspot.com**.

About Brent Chitwood

rent Chitwood lives in North-east Georgia. He is a graduate of Ringling School of Art in Sarasota, Florida, with a BFA degree. He worked in outdoor advertising for twenty years, painting scenic outdoor displays. He has been married to Becky for 31 years. They have two daughters and four grandchildren.

Connect With Brent...

Visit Brent's Web site at **www.rembrentart.com** or email **chitwoodbrent@bellsouth.net.**

If You're a Fan of This Book, Please Tell Others…

- Write about *Unwrapping His Presence* on your blog, Twitter, MySpace, and Facebook page.
- Suggest *Unwrapping His Presence* to friends.
- When you're in a bookstore, ask them if they carry the book. The book is available through all major distributors so any bookstore that does not have *Unwrapping His Presence* in stock can easily order it.
- Write a positive review of *Unwrapping His Presence* on www.amazon.com.
- Send my publisher, HigherLife Publishing, suggestions on Web sites, conferences, and events you know of where this book could be offered. Their contact information is listed is below:

HigherLife Publishing
400 Fontana Circle
Building 1 – Suite 105
Oviedo, Florida 32765
Phone: (407) 563-4806
Email: media@ahigherlife.com

- Purchase additional copies to give away as gifts. My contact information is listed on page 100.